Around
the
Cross

Discovery House Publishers

Books, music, and videos that feed the soul with the Word of God

Box 3566 Grand Rapids, MI 49501

The Friendship Connection

Around the Cross

Norene Antin, M.A.

Discovery House Publishers is affiliated with RBC Ministries, Grand Rapids, Michigan 49512

Discovery House books are distributed to the trade exclusively by Barbour Publishing, Inc., Uhrichsville, Ohio 44683

All Scripture quotations, unless otherwise indicated, are from the HOLY BIBLE, NEW INTERNATIONAL VERSION® (NIV®). Copyright © 1973, 1978, 1984 by International Bible Society. Used by permission of Zondervan Publishing House.

Songs used by permission of Word Publishing, Nashville, Tennessee.

In some cases, names and details have been changed in the "Modern Day Story" out of respect for and in protection of individuals.

Library of Congress Cataloging-in-Publication Data

Antin, Norene.
    Around the cross / by Norene Antin.
        p. cm. -- (The friendship connection)
    ISBN 1-57293-075-6
    1. Christian women--Religious life. 2. Bible. N.T.--Biography. 3. Friendship--Religious aspects--Christianity.   I. Title.
    BV4527 .A57 2001
    248.8'43--dc21

                                                                                            2001028320

Printed in the United States of America.

01 02 03 04 05 06 07 / CHG / 7 6 5 4 3 2 1

contents . . .

acknowledgments . . .

Thanks be to God who continues to show His awesome power daily, especially by enabling me to connect with Himself and with others.

Secondly, thanks to my husband, Ernie, and my daughter, Vanessa, who are a joy to live with. They reflect the grace of God daily to me. Both are outstanding encouragers. They, along with my sons and their families, continue to melt my heart with the realization that God has loaned them to *me*.

Others who have contributed significantly behind the scenes through faithful friendship, as well as through encouraging me, advising me, and holding me accountable: Carole Veitch, Mary Butcher, Heather Webb, Annie Hurley, Cheryle Hamilton, and Sandi Nightingale.

Rosalie Harkless has again touched my heart and soul with her Christ-like spirit and unique talents. She is a true artist and professional, whose expert work I admire and thank God for.

I am thankful as well for Carol Holquist and Tim Gustafson of Discovery House Publishers—for the kindness they have shown and for the wonderful assistance they have given me.

how to use this study guide . . .

This Bible study guide was created to facilitate the moving of the Spirit in women's hearts. It is the second in *The Friendship Connection* series designed for use by the network of Friendship Circle® International. This ministry to women was founded in 1989 in Renton, Washington, to help women develop friendships with the Lord Jesus and with each other and to testify of His grace.

The guide is rich with Scripture references and quotations, application notes, and appropriate discussion themes. When used in a group setting, it becomes an excellent tool for growth and bonding. To gain maximum benefit from this study you will need *your Bible, sensitivity to the Holy Spirit, and an open heart.*

Each chapter consists of seven sections: The Bible lesson can be read either before or during the group meeting; "A Modern Day Story" helps the reader to relate the Bible lesson to today's culture; "Sharing Our Hearts" provides discussion starters which replace Bible study questions typical of a study guide and are intended to stimulate group discussion; "A Change of Heart" is a section devoted to summarizing and applying the lesson; "Walk the Word" gives practical ideas for living out what has been learned and taken to heart; ample space is given to a "Notes" section for the reader to record her thoughts and insights; and "Hearing His Heart" provides an additional Scripture passage for reading and meditation for each day between group meetings.

The final section of the guide is a prayer journal to record petitions as well as praises for answers received—a tool that will help you to come face-to-face with the grace of the Lord Jesus Christ.

If you would like more information about Friendship Circle® International, please contact: Friendship Circle® International, P.O. Box 2062, Renton, WA 98056.

Introduction

The theme of the cross has always fascinated me. Perhaps the main reason is that I am far from understanding it completely. Frequently I have asked myself, "How could something so horrible provide something so wonderful?" I do not know how. I just know that it does.

I have also asked myself, "What does the cross mean to me today?" For someone like myself who has grown up in the church with a preacher dad, graduated from Bible school and seminary, and been involved in various forms of ministry all of her life, what tangible, day-to-day relevance does the cross have anyway?

I am sad to admit that for many years it had no relevance for me. I faithfully and dutifully did the church thing, always depending on God, of course, to help me. I prayed a lot, and participated in, wrote and taught Bible studies. But to look inside my life at the ways I was grieving God or others was a foreign concept to me. To get out of myself and into loving accountable relationships with others was something I had never even considered. Those actions were reserved for the "obvious" sinner—the addict, you know. To offer *more* than just a token service to the Lord, consisting of raising my family and teaching a Bibly study, never entered my mind. It was not until I had come face-to-face with death, as I lay on a gurney being wheeled into an operating room, that I realized that I had been living life *badly*. That day I vowed that if I came out of surgery still on this side of heaven, I would live my life differently. I would live life *better*, that is, with eternity's values in view.

The cross is all about eternal values. It is about living life for Jesus every day. It is about repentance and changing your ways so that you can be a better wife, mother, daughter, sister, co-worker, and friend, because you perceive, in a tiny way, the massive love of God. It is about saying, "Not my brother, not my sister, but it's me, O Lord, standing in the need of prayer. I am the sinner in need of your grace."

From the ushering in of this revolutionary concept of Good News through John the Baptist (Lesson 1) to the friends of Jesus who line His pathway as He approaches the cross (Lessons 2-5) to the passing of the baton to Paul (Lesson 6), the cross is prominent. It must be. There is no real life apart from dying to self and living in loving communion and community. There is only existence—a depressing, boring drudgery at best. The cross gives hope that God will make miracles out of messes. He touches and we are transformed. He calls, and we are connected. He reaches and we are rescued, redeemed, and revived.

I know. He has done this for me and continues to do so. I pray that He will do the same for you, as you journey with confidence in the One who is actively pursuing you in order to lavish you with His love. *May you see Jesus like you have never seen Him before.* And then, in seeing Him and being touched by Him, may you "*be* Jesus" to others. *"By this all men will know that you are my disciples, if you love one another"* (John 13:35).

My friend, we are all equal at the cross. Let us walk together to be better, for we are confident that the best is yet to come!

Lorene

CHAPTER 1

John the Baptist: A Different Voice

A Friend Brings Harmony

O To Be Like Thee

O to be like Thee! Blessed Redeemer,
This is my constant longing and prayer;
Gladly I'll forfeit all of earth's treasures,
Jesus, Thy perfect likeness to wear.

O to be like Thee—full of compassion,
Loving, forgiving, tender and kind.
Helping the helpless, cheering the fainting,
Seeking the wandering sinner to find.

O to be like Thee while I am pleading,
Pour out Thy Spirit; fill with Thy love.
Make me a temple meet for Thy dwelling.
Fit me for life and heaven above.

Chorus:
O to be like Thee! O to be like Thee!
Blessed Redeemer, pure as Thou art!
Come in Thy sweetness, come in Thy fullness.
Stamp Thine own image deep on my heart.

—Thomas O. Chisholm

Scripture Reading: Luke 1 and Luke 3:1-20

*I*t is nothing new to any of us that people can be as different from one another as night and day, and this can create problems. A majority of husbands and wives know this to be the case, and our divorce statistics prove it. Even apart from marriage, on the friendship level, it is sometimes a real challenge to get along with someone we think of as a dear friend. As hard as we try, we do see life differently and this can often create sparks of misunderstanding. So what is needed to help the sparks fizzle and to live peacefully with those we love? A look at the prophet John the Baptist, so very different from anyone else of his day, can provide us insight.

John the Baptist is indeed different. He lives in a desert, eats grasshoppers and honey, and clothes himself with camel's hair and a leather belt. Most people live in the city; eat fish, meat, bread, and potatoes; and shop at Peter's Friendly Fish Market and Lydia's Designer Mall. In today's world, John's lifestyle could be equated to that of a recluse living far from any town or city and never eating at McDonald's or shopping at Costco or JC Penney. Can you imagine?

The Spirit Sings

There is a reason that John is different. His father, Zechariah, belongs to the priesthood and his mother, Elizabeth, also comes from the priestly line of Aaron. They are the only set of parents mentioned in the Bible who are both filled with the Holy Spirit (Luke 1:41,67). What is particularly noteworthy is that they conceive a baby who is also filled with the Holy Spirit already in his mother's womb (Luke 1:15).

To be filled with the Spirit sets one apart as very unique and chosen for God's purposes. What a high privilege that is. Few are given this wonderful gift prior to the day of Pentecost. So this baby's Spirit-filled parents do not follow the custom of naming him after his father; rather, in obedience to God, they call him *John,* which means "God is gracious." John is appropriately named because those who receive God's Spirit are granted an extra portion of grace. With the arrival of this gracious baby, there is great joy and his dad sings and prophesies (Luke 1:67-79). The stage has been set for a remarkable prophet who will *"make ready a people prepared for the Lord"* (Luke 1:17).

First, however, John needs to make himself ready. That in itself is unusual, because the practice of many of the religious leaders of his day is to tell others how to live and not necessarily to concern themselves with modeling the message they are teaching. So as John lives in the desert far away from the limelight (Luke 1:80), in this place of solitude and simplicity, he comes to know, believe in, and practice the message he has been called to preach. He learns submission to God's purposes when life is tough. Following God's Spirit to live in the desert, he learns to put God first and himself second, mastering the art of playing second fiddle in preparation for Jesus' appearance on the scene. He learns to do things for God's approval alone. No one is around to applaud, praise, promote, or pay him. Indeed he learns to hear God's voice and to tune out all the voices of the world that might want to exalt him or urge him to defend himself.

John becomes the one voice in the wilderness, not in the synagogue, who calls God's people back to Himself through a *"baptism of repentance for the forgiveness of sins"* (Luke 3:3). God longs for intimacy with His people, but sin prevents this relationship.

It is time to become serious about sin, God, and the grace He is about to usher in through His Son.

John's is a simple message from a simple man who voluntarily relinquishes his personal rights. Those include the rights to priesthood, to live comfortably, to be with his family, to dress stylishly, to eat like everyone else, and to be liked by other people. He willingly gives up his rights to be somebody in the world's eyes in order to be somebody in God's eyes—a prophet, and even greater, a friend of Jesus—as he humbly walks the talk and stays in harmony with the Spirit.

Friends Sing Each Other's Praises

A friend of Jesus he is, even though the two are so different. John lives in solitude in the desert and fasts often; Jesus lives in the city and attends many social gatherings. John has never been a guest speaker in the synagogue; Jesus regularly fills this role. Although John baptizes many in water, Jesus does not. John sees only the miracle of a changed heart; Jesus daily performs miracles that are visible to all.

Although they are so unalike, and misunderstanding could easily arise between them, it does not. In fact, the opposite is true, one reason being that their attitudes are ones of mutual respect and love. Jesus speaks highly of John when He says, *"There has not risen anyone greater than John the Baptist"*(Matthew 11:11). John could have a desire to outshine or compete with Jesus. He could nurture hurt feelings because he is not chosen by Jesus as a disciple or guaranteed a place of honor next to Him in heaven. But his love for Jesus prevails, and in humility he announces, *"One more powerful than I will come, the thongs of whose sandals I am not worthy to untie"* (Luke 3:16).

A second reason for the harmony between them is that both are truly filled with the Spirit (Luke 1:15; 4:1). When one is filled with the Spirit, one's mind is set on pleasing God rather than on satisfying self-promoting desires. In fact, John goes so far as to say, *"He must become greater; I must become less"* (John 3:30). That is exactly what happens because shortly after that John is imprisoned and later killed.

Jesus is not seeking to elevate Himself either. He voluntarily leaves behind all the riches and comforts of heaven, comes to live on this fallen planet, and *"[makes] Himself nothing, taking the very nature of a servant"* (Philippians 2:7). He is not looking for esteem or approval from the world, nor does He receive it. What He does receive are whippings for His words, mocking for His miracles, and, ultimately, torturous treatment on a cruel cross intended for a criminal. But He also receives His Father's approval, and that is the one reality that matters most to any servant of God.

A Look at a Singing Servant Today

What exactly does it mean to be a servant? As a true servant you simply and quietly serve, doing your best, without announcing what you are doing. Often you are the one to ask, "How may I help you?" and then you actually follow through and do whatever it takes. Being a servant means that you allow the other person to have first choice, and you take the leftovers, if there are any. It means being the first to say "I'm sorry." It means trying to identify how God is conforming you to His Son's image, rather than nursing your wounds and defending your rights over and over again. It means forgiving the hurt and pain because God forgives you for a lot more. It means desiring God's will more than your own comfort, convenience, or preference. It means being honest enough to say, "*I* need to change," rather than focusing on how *someone else* needs to change. It means loving whether or not the love is reciprocated. It means letting go of your pride and accepting truth from godly lips, no matter how painful it is to hear—and then acting on it. And it means singing in the night.

Having a servant's attitude does bring about harmony. To live harmoniously is to live differently. But to live differently costs. It costs dearly. It cost these two men everything, including their lives. Both realized that their lives were about giving and serving where God wanted them to be, and not about shouting, withdrawing, self-promoting, or getting their own way.

Heaven Sings

Both John and Jesus were in tune with the heavenly Father. When we tune up to match His heart and obey the Spirit by focusing on eternal things, we are in harmony with others too. Just as in music there can be no harmony unless someone sings or plays the lower notes, so in life someone needs to take the lesser role, giving up rehearsing all the sour notes of criticism and contentiousness and beginning faithfully to build up and appreciate the gift of the other person. This is not to imply that hard words are never to be spoken or that confrontation should never take place. The messages of both of these men showed that was not the case. Truth must be declared, but it must always be cushioned with love.

Excuse me, but is that a song I hear? Won't you join me, friend? It sounds as though Someone is singing with us. *"He will rejoice over you with singing"* (Zephaniah 3:17).

A Modern Day Story
Judy: A Friend Who Brings Harmony

The other day I called my friend, Judy, to ask about her secret for getting along so well with her husband and other church members, even though life has not been easy for her. I see her often taking the more humble role, indeed playing second fiddle. Here is what she told me:

"I have decided that it is the Lord I am working for, and it is He to whom I will have to answer for all my actions. Sometimes I really do want to do things my own way, and I grumble and growl. But I see that that doesn't work. It doesn't fly. So I need to just move on and know my pay-off is not from people or from my husband. It is from the Lord. I am trusting He hears my heart and will reward me in His time. Although I know I am not first in my husband's life right now, and other women tell me I am supposed to have first place, the fact is I don't and so I keep trusting God and serving Him."

As her friend I see how, with her gifts of encouragement and service, Judy beautifully meets the needs of others, including those of her husband. She is a great inspiration to many of us.

Sharing Our Hearts

Discussion Starters

Reflect on the following thoughts we will discuss together. Take particular note of those that strike a chord with you and add notes in the margin about them.

1. Think of a friend whose company you enjoy. In what ways does this friend help to create the harmony between you?

    ❑ compliments me

    ❑ asks about me

    ❑ prays for me

    ❑ refrains from withdrawing or criticizing when I disappoint

    ❑ other: _____

    _____

    _____

    _____

2. Name some things people can do to create harmony in their own homes.

    ❑ Build each other up.

    ❑ Take truly relaxing vacations as a family or couple.

    ❑ Laugh together more often.

    ❑ Help each other around the house.

    ❑ Pray often for and with one another.

    ❑ Apologize when they've hurt each other.

    ❑ other: _____

    _____

_____

_____

3. The older we get, the harder it is to change. Name some things you can do to help facilitate change.

❏ Admit my need for change.

❏ Ask God for help because "*with God all things are possible*" (Matthew 19:26).

❏ Ask a friend for help—there's strength in having a kindred spirit.

❏ Thank both God and my friends for their past help.

❏ Be patient and persevering; don't give up trying.

❏ other: _____

_____

_____

_____

4. What do you appreciate most in one who has a servant's attitude?

❏ does things without being asked

❏ grateful for just a simple thanks

❏ doesn't like to be in the lime-light

❏ not bossy

❏ not picky or critical

❏ other _____

_____

_____

_____

5. Jesus Christ declared that the greatest in the kingdom of God is the one who humbly serves (Matthew 20:26). Why do you not naturally choose to serve others?

❏ selfishness: I like to have my own needs met first.

❏ laziness: I assume that there is someone else who will do it.

❏ lack of confidence: I'm not sure I can do it well.

❏ fear of criticism: I may be misunderstood or my actions may not be met with approval.

❏ ignorance: I do not realize how much Christ has served me.

❏ other _____

_____

_____

A Change of Heart
Lesson Summary and Application

One main thought I have gleaned from the lesson:

_____

_____

_____

One application of this lesson to my life: With God's help . . .

❏ I will seek harmony in my relationship with_____

_____

❏ I will be more of a servant to others, rather than expecting them to serve me.

❏ I will choose second place more often.

❑ other _____

_____

_____

_____

_____

Walk the Word

❑ Call a friend you have not talked with for awhile. Be intent on listening rather than talking about yourself.

❑ Ask your pastor, church leader, or teacher, "Is there something I can do to help you?"

❑ If you are a mom or a grandma, help your children or grandchildren pick up their toys. Enjoy chatting with them as you do.

Notes

_____

_____

_____

_____

_____

_____

_____

_____

Hearing His Heart

The following verses on this week's topic, "A Friend Brings Harmony," are given for deepening your love for the Lord and for others. Space is provided after each verse for you to record your thoughts.

WEEK 1

Monday

Romans 12:16

"Live in _____ with one another. Do not be proud, but be willing to associate with people of low position. Do not be conceited."

_____

_____

_____

Tuesday

1 Peter 3:8

"All of you, live in _____ with one another; be sympathetic, love as brothers, be compassionate and humble."

_____

_____

_____

Wednesday

Proverbs 20:3

"It is to a man's honor to avoid _____ , but every fool is quick to quarrel."

_____

_____

_____

Thursday

Philippians 2:3-4

"Do nothing out of selfish ambition or vain conceit, but in humility consider others better than yourselves. Each of you should look not only to your own interests, but also to the interests of _____ ."

_____

_____

_____

Friday

1 Corinthians 13:4-7

"Love is patient, love is kind. It does not envy, it does not boast, it is not proud. It is not rude, it is not _____ , it is not easily angered, it keeps no record of wrongs. Love does not delight in evil but rejoices with the truth. It always protects, always trusts, always hopes, always perseveres."

_____

_____

_____

WEEK 2

Monday

Romans 12:10

"Be devoted to one another in _____ . Honor one another above yourselves."

_____

_____

_____

Tuesday

Ephesians 5:19-21

"Speak to one another with psalms, hymns and spiritual songs.

Sing and make music in your heart to the Lord, always giving thanks to God the Father for everything, in the name of our Lord Jesus Christ. _____
out of reverence for Christ."

_____
_____
_____

Wednesday

2 Timothy 2:24

"The Lord's servant must not _____ ; instead he must be kind to everyone, able to teach, not resentful."

_____
_____
_____

Thursday

Romans 15:7

"Accept one another, then, just as Christ accepted you, in order to _____ ."

_____
_____
_____

Friday

James 3:17

"The wisdom that comes from heaven is first of all pure; then peace-loving, considerate, _____ , full of mercy and good fruit, impartial and sincere."

_____
_____
_____

Mary, Martha & Lazarus: The Triumphant Teammates

A Friend Feels With You

I Will Sing of My Redeemer

I *will sing of my Redeemer and His wondrous love to me,*
On the cruel cross He suffered, from the curse to set me free.

I will tell the wondrous story, how my lost estate to save,
In His boundless love and mercy, He the ransom freely gave.

I will praise my dear Redeemer, His triumphant power I'll tell,
How the victory He giveth over sin and death and hell.

I will sing of my Redeemer and His heavenly love to me;
He from death to life hath brought me, Son of God with Him to be.

> *Chorus:*
> *Sing, O sing of my Redeemer*
> *With His blood He purchased me;*
> *On the cross He sealed my pardon,*
> *Paid the debt and made me free.*

—Phillip P. Bliss

Scripture Reading: John 11:1-44

ow do you respond when you hear that a friend has cancer, has just lost a loved one or has been told that her spouse wants a divorce? What words can you say that will help at such a heartrending time? What can you do that will make a difference? A look at a visit Jesus makes to a grieving family, the Mary and Martha household, offers insight on how to be a better friend who empathizes with and helps others in their time of crisis.

As the story opens, word is sent by the sisters, dear friends of Jesus, that their brother Lazarus is gravely ill, even to the point of death. When Jesus receives the painful message, *"Lord, the one you love is sick"* (John 11:3), He stays where He is, purposely not responding immediately to this emergency situation. In fact, it appears that these favored friends of Jesus are not top priority to Him at this time, because He does not drop what He is doing, slip into his Nike Air sandals, and sprint without delay in their direction.

What He does instead seems like a huge mistake. He stays put for two days longer. Did you get that? He does *nothing*. He who can do anything does *nothing*! And He who has helped thousands of others is apparently too busy to rescue His own dear friends in their hour of need. Or so it would seem.

Unless, of course, He is up to something else. Could His agenda involve more than "just" rescuing people? Might He also be about resurrecting? *Resurrecting*? What is that? His friends are about to hear and see that He who seemingly does nothing in reality will do *everything* in His own perfect time.

Love Speaks and Weeps

As the story continues, Jesus makes His delayed appearance at the grieving household after Lazarus has been entombed for four days. The delay has given the sisters ample time to stew, and upon seeing Jesus individually, each greets Him with the identical words: *"Lord, if you had been here, my brother would not have died"* (John 11:21, 32). That's a very honest statement. Paraphrased, one might say, "You were supposed to show up sooner, but you didn't."

Honesty is a quality Jesus desires, and His individually tailored response to each of them is worth noting. He does not dismiss or correct the sisters. They have forged a friendship with Him over time and know Him to be incredibly accepting of whatever they say or do. So true to His Spirit of unconditional love, He responds to Martha with the amazing statement of truth that He Himself is *"the resurrection and the life"* (John 11:25). To Mary, who falls at His feet, a familiar spot for her (see Luke 10:39), He responds from His heart by simply weeping along with her (John 11:35).

What a beautiful picture of entering into the suffering of others who grieve—Jesus caring enough to speak words of encouragement to those who rebuke Him and to weep with those who weep. He feels their pain and does not make light of it or remove Himself from it. First, He *listens*, and then He *responds*. He who is deeply troubled Himself (John 11:33), perhaps in part because of the nearness of His own crucifixion, is committed to caring for His friends. This is an excellent example for us to follow as we journey with our friends through difficult and sad times.

Teammates Needed

But Jesus does something more that is significant. So must we, if we are to see God's resurrection power at work in our own lives and in the lives of others who hurt.

In a state of heavy-heartedness, Jesus approaches the tomb where Lazarus is buried and asks for some assistance in rolling back the stone laid across the entrance. Jesus, as God, could have accomplished this by Himself or even recruited angelic assistance, but He rejects these methods. He selects these humble, grieving mourners to be His teammates, in spite of the protests of practical, forthright Martha (John 11:39). This sister is known for feeling free to speak her mind (Luke 10:40), and this time her mind is concerned with her nose and what it is about to smell. But that is not Jesus' concern, and He is not about to let the gravestone gather any moss.

As the stone is rolled away, Jesus does not barge in. No, in His gentle manner He does something much more appropriate, the kind of action that is His trademark and badge of authenticity. He looks up and *speaks to His Father*, and then His gentleness gives way to firmness as He speaks in a loud voice, summoning Lazarus to come out of the tomb, "Lazarus, come out" (John 11:43).

Jesus can speak and act with authority because He recognizes the One True Authority and understands what His Father wants to do at this time of sorrow. Amazingly, the dead man stirs, revives, and responds, and then the practical Jesus instructs His teammates at the tomb to remove Lazarus's grave clothes so that their brother may be free to love and be loved again by his earthly family. That is resurrection power at its finest.

Teammates Become Soul Mates

Jesus' presence and actions make a difference in the lives of this grieving household. However, we are not Jesus and cannot change others' circumstances. We do not have the power to raise others from the dead physically, but we do have ability as a teammate with the Lord to raise the discouraged spirits of others when they are "dying" inside because of their sorrow or grief. With the help of the Holy Spirit who reveals God's awesome love for us, we can tap into God's unlimited power to help us to love and feel with our friends (Ephesians 4:18). As we *listen, pray,* and *partner* with God with clear purpose and direction, we can see His resurrection power at work in our everyday lives. We can also be teammates, perhaps even privileged soul mates, who participate with God in the rekindling in others of faith, hope, and love for God and His people and we too can watch a miracle of resurrection unfold.

A Modern Day Story
Joan: A Friend Who Feels With Others

Joan, a friend of mine who had lost her mother, told me, *"I saw in a new way how God heals our broken hearts:* He uses friends and family to come alongside of us. *When He said He will 'bind up our wounds,' I visualized a gaping wound that will not close. You have probably had a cut on a knuckle or a finger where it would not close by itself. You must squeeze it together and then hold it together with a bandage on top of that.*

"God brings our friends alongside and they are the ones who hold the wound shut or 'bind it up.' Then, God is the One who does the ultimate healing. *If we are not able to use the proper bandage, our cut will stay open for days. So, if these special people in our lives do not make themselves available, or do not listen to what God is telling them to do, the wound in our life will remain open for a longer time. In time, it will eventually heal, but there will be a wide scar.*

"God does not ask us to do huge and spectacular things. He doesn't ask us to do miracles or invent a cure for an illness, or solve the person's problem. He just asks us to come alongside of them and help hold their wound together. *You might think you can't do anything big, but if it is just a call, a hug, a visit, a card, prayers for them, it helps the person feel they are not alone and* there is someone who cares. *While it is God's love that is holding us up, it helps to actually see people who are doing these little acts of love."*

I have been encouraged with Joan's touch in many lives. She excels in giving practically and meaningfully.

Sharing Our Hearts

Discussion Starters

Reflect on the following thoughts we will discuss together. Take particular note of those that strike a chord with you and add notes in the margin about them.

1. Sometimes when a friend comes to you with a problem, you may feel overwhelmed and think that you have nothing to offer. Why do you not help more?

   ❏ I am in shock as well and I am not confident that I can help.

   ❏ I do not want to give up control of my time, schedule, or money.

   ❏ I have not prayed and listened to what God wants me to do.

   ❏ I do not see that I am God's teammate along with other members of the church.

   ❏ other: _____

   _____

   _____

   _____

   _____

   _____

2. The same resurrection power that is in Jesus is in us. Read Romans 8:11. What significance does this passage have for your life today?

   ❏ I can do the "impossible" with God's help.

   ❏ God can raise me up from my own broken or dying existence to a life of giving and nurturing others.

❏ I do not have to let anyone or anything defeat, discourage, or destroy me.

❏ I can start fresh today in my commitment to God and to

_____

❏ Because I am dearly loved by God, He gives me all of Himself. I can then live, thanking Him through caring words and deeds.

❏ other: _____

_____

_____

_____

3. When someone came alongside you and felt your pain, how did you respond?

❏ I softened my heart and began to trust in a new way.

❏ I did the same for someone else.

❏ I thanked God for His love and didn't become bitter over the unwelcome event.

❏ I wept because _____

_____

❏ I drew nearer to God and found Him drawing nearer to me.

❏ other: _____

_____

_____

_____

4. Those who have stood by the bedside of a dying loved one have shared some important truths they have learned from that experience. Can you add to their thoughts?

❏ I was sorrowful, but I was comforted by God's presence.

❏ I experienced God's presence in the love of friends and family who visited, prayed, or brought a meal to my home.

❏ I experienced God's peace as I prayed, sang, and read Scripture.

❏ I never thought I could live through it, but I did, and I saw God giving me the grace to do it.

❏ The experience helped me to examine my own life. I know that I too will die someday, and I began asking how I could live with eternity in view.

❏ other: _____

_____

_____

_____

_____

5. What is an effective way to pray for those who are hurting?

❏ that God would comfort and encourage them

❏ that their friends and family would be sensitive to their needs

❏ that they would be strengthened moment by moment

❏ that they would sense God's nearness

❏ that they would be able to express themselves to someone else who cares

❏ other: _____

_____

_____

_____

_____

A Change of Heart

Lesson Summary and Application

One main thought I have gleaned from the lesson:

❏ When a friend "feels" with me the burden is lighter.

❏ other: _____

_____

_____

_____

One application of this lesson to my life: With God's help . . .

❏ I will feel with my grieving friend _____
by doing the following: _____

_____

_____

_____

❏ I will become a better team player in God's family of faith.

❏ I will live more responsibly and unselfishly by: _____

_____

_____

_____

_____

❏ other: _____

_____

_____

_____

_____

Walk the Word

- ❑ Be available to just spend time with someone who is hurting.
- ❑ Call, e-mail, or visit someone who has experienced a loss within the past year. Ask how she is doing now.
- ❑ Encourage someone who is leaving the old for something new (such as a new job, home, career, ministry, or school).

Notes

_____

_____

_____

_____

_____

_____

_____

_____

_____

_____

_____

_____

_____

_____

Hearing His Heart

The following verses on this week's topic, "A Friend Feels With You," are given for deepening your love for the Lord and for others. Space is provided after each verse for you to record your thoughts.

WEEK 1

Monday

Colossian 3:12

"As God's chosen people, holy and dearly loved, clothe yourselves with compassion, _____ , humility, gentleness and patience."

_____

_____

_____

Tuesday

Luke 10:33-34

"A Samaritan ... took pity on him. He went to him and bandaged his wounds, pouring on oil and wine. Then he put the man on his own donkey, took him to an inn and _____ ."

_____

_____

_____

Wednesday

2 Corinthians 7:6

"God, who _____ the downcast, comforted us by the coming of Titus."

_____

_____

_____

Thursday

Ephesians 4:32

*"Be kind and _____ to one
another, _____ each other, just as in Christ
God _____."*

_____

_____

_____

Friday

Proverbs 31:10,25-26

*"A wife of _____ who
can find? She is worth far more than rubies.... She is clothed with
strength and dignity; she can laugh at the days to come. She speaks
with wisdom, and faithful instruction is on her tongue."*

_____

_____

_____

WEEK 2

Monday

Romans 12:9-10,13,15

*"Love must be sincere. Hate what is evil; cling to what is good. Be
devoted to one another in _____ .
_____ one another above yourselves.... Share with God's
people who are in need. Practice _____ .
... Rejoice with those who rejoice; mourn with those who mourn."*

_____

_____

_____

Tuesday

Zechariah 7:9

"... show _____ *and compassion to one another."*

_____

_____

_____

Wednesday

Galatians 6:2

"Carry each other's _____ *."*

_____

_____

_____

Thursday

John 15:13

"Greater love has no one than this, that he lay down his _____
for his friends."

_____

_____

_____

Friday

Ephesians 5:1

*"Be imitators of God, therefore, as dearly loved children and live a
life of love, just as Christ loved us and gave himself up for us as a
fragrant offering and* _____ *."*

_____

_____

_____

CHAPTER 3

One Thief
Captured by Grace

A Friend Remembers

Softly and Tenderly

*Softly and tenderly Jesus is calling,
Calling for you and for me;
See, on the portals He's waiting and watching,
Watching for you and for me.*

*Why should we tarry when Jesus is pleading,
Pleading for you and for me?
Why should we linger and heed not His mercies,
Mercies for you and for me?*

*Time is now fleeting, the moments are passing,
Passing from you and from me;
Shadows are gathering, death's night is coming,
Coming for you and for me.*

*O for the wonderful love He has promised,
Promised for you and for me!
Though we have sinned, He has mercy and pardon,
Pardon for you and for me.*

Chorus:
*Come home, come home,
Ye who are weary, come home;
Earnestly, tenderly, Jesus is calling,
Calling, O sinner, come home!"*

—Will L. Thompson

Scripture Reading: Luke 23:32-33,39-43 and Mark 15:27-32

ife gets busy and we often find that there is not enough time to do the things we want to do or see the people we want to see. Sometimes we do not even remember important dates or events as we get caught up with life's hectic demands. Does that matter? Is it any big deal when we *do* remember? A snapshot from the lives of three men, all of whom are facing imminent death, demonstrates clearly the importance of remembering as Grace comes knocking on their door.

A Thief Is Punished

Our story opens with each of the three men enduring crucifixion on a cross. There has never been a more grotesque form of execution for a criminal. Everything about it is inhumane. Most of us are familiar with the story as it relates to one of the men, Jesus, the Son of God. And we are moved beyond words by the nature and extent of His suffering for us. Our response is appropriate. We should be stirred because this single act represents the greatest sacrifice and expression of love in the history of the world. Recognizing that Jesus' suffering was endured for us personally is absolutely life-changing. It has been so for many of us, and it will certainly be so on this particular day for one who is known as a thief.

As grace would have it, this criminal occupies a place of "prominence" next to Jesus. He is one of two who has been chosen for that very spot on this memorable day. There are many who have requested to sit with Jesus on His right or left hand when He comes into His kingdom. But no one is standing in line for a spot next to Him on this particular day when He is about to be slaughtered before the world's eyes. In fact, his eleven remaining disciples have all deserted Him in terror (Mark 14:50).

Now who would have envisioned that the coveted places of "honor" would be given to two common criminals? Such an idea would have been unthinkable from the human perspective. But the God whose name is Grace would think of doing precisely this. And so Grace makes a "home" visit to a vile thief—a captive audience, as he hangs suspended in agony, shame, and guilt on a cross he has earned by his actions. So has his cohort in crime, the one who hangs shamefully on the opposite side of Jesus. This other sinner will choose not to acknowledge his guilt, and he will consequently be unable to recognize Grace's visit that day.

Somebody Notices

We do not know the names of these two robbers. Rather than name either one of them, let's keep it that way, lest we get too close to them. They are, after all, nobodies in the world's eyes. *Nobodies.* Jesus, who is the ultimate *Somebody*, is being crucified between two nobodies.

How utterly humiliating—unless of course, He sees it differently. Does Jesus see that they are somebodies, too? Does He also see that He Himself is a nobody in the eyes of the religious leaders who have rejected and condemned Him and ordered His crucifixion? Will He in His dying hour continue to elevate others and identify completely with the "worst" of sinners?

The Lord Jesus has *created* these two men. He hasn't wished for them to grow up to be robbers and no-namers. No, He has desired that each of them know what a Very Important Person he is in God's eyes. But one cannot know he is truly a somebody until he admits he is a nobody apart from a visit from Grace.

And so Grace continues to invite. From lips that are parched and bleeding, Grace speaks with the last ounce of energy available. *"Father, forgive them,"* Grace pleads. Then Grace stretches, going the distance, and then some: not cursing the darkness, but lighting a candle; not shouting, "You failure!" but softly whispering, "You're forgiven!" Grace's focus is, as always, to triumph over evil.

A Concert of Disgrace

Certainly on this day, evil abounds. All three men are dying. Jesus, the Creator, hangs between the criminals while barbed words are flung back and forth between the two of them (see Matthew 27:44; Mark 15:32). It seems as though the lacerations by the soldiers are not enough, and so Jesus is being whipped with words by those on the ground as well as by His fellow sufferers.

A stereo effect is achieved in this concert of curses as first one and then the other hurls insults at their Creator Redeemer. Then there is a swelling crescendo of discord as those below bellow up at Him more curses, slander, and lies.

A Symphony of Love

The challenge to Jesus to *"Save yourself"* (Luke 23:37) is the most popular phrase of biting insult. But saving Himself is not foremost on Jesus' mind. What is on His mind are people—you, me, and those robbers. Our Savior's lavish, outrageous, inexhaustible, redemptive, forgiving love keeps us close to Him in thought and heart, even in His hour of physical and spiritual agony. For He knows that we all have something in common. We could never, even in a trillion years, save ourselves.

Did you hear that? *We cannot save ourselves!* All our noble efforts, our money, our church, our prayers, our Bible study, our family, or our friends cannot get us into heaven. They will get us nowhere for they mean nothing to our Creator God who has made it clear that there is only one way into heaven. Jesus said, *"I am the way, and the truth and the life"* (John 14:6). His blood, and only His blood, provides the way.

And Jesus, with love dripping from every bloody pore, so completely identifies with sinful man that even He *cannot* save Himself!

Captured by Love

Jesus on His incredible, incomprehensible, unrepeatable mission of mercy for others cannot save Himself but instead does what He knows He can do. He pours out His love and grace. Both thieves hear Him; one reacts with more insults, but the other responds. Amazingly, this hardened criminal about to enter eternity allows his heart and mind to be softened, reaches out to the Savior with something other than curses and acknowledges his own sin.

Humbly, he does not ask for a place in heaven. He simply wants to be remembered. What does that say about his life on earth? Is he a forgotten son, brother, or husband? Has nobody paid attention to him? Has he had to steal to be noticed? To be talked to? Has there been no one standing by to comfort him? Now One is talking to him who will forever *want* to remember him. This common criminal has been blessed with a personal relationship with the God of the universe, a relationship that he does not initiate—but neither does he ignore the knock of Grace on his heart's door. Grace has amazingly come to take him home, assuring him, *"I tell you the truth, today you will be with me in paradise!"* (Luke 23:43).

Once more Jesus identifies with the robber. What it means to be remembered is fresh in His own mind. During His very last meal with his best friends, less than twenty-four hours earlier, He had asked to be remembered. At that solemn and sorrowful time, He had shared with them broken bread and a cup of wine, symbolizing His coming act of pouring out His life for them, and He had instructed them to, *"Do this in remembrance of me"* (Luke 22:19). Jesus knows the eternal importance to them—and to us—of remembering His sacrifice. If his best friends do not remember, then who will? Will He have lived and died in vain?

Always Worth Remembering

Shortly afterward, Jesus breathes His last, and His mission of redemption is completed. But His daily remembering of us never ends. His love never changes, and we are always on His mind. Grace still makes house calls, usually when we are at our worst and when we least expect Him.

What's that knocking I hear? Could that be Grace? Come in! Salvation? For me? How can this be? Grace remembering me? Amazing Grace always wants to have the last word, you know. And this one is well worth remembering: *"For it is by grace you have been saved, through faith—and this not from yourselves, it is the gift of God—not by works, so that no one can boast"* (Ephesians 2:8-9).

A Modern Day Story
Donna: A Friend Who Remembered

A few years after our Friendship Circle® began meeting, one of our members died in an auto accident. Because she was the first of us to be ushered into the presence of God, we were especially impacted, and we recognized that she had been given an honored place. So when the holidays came around the next year, we wanted to remember her. We recalled that she had particularly loved helping the needy, and so we began an outreach to the community and the church family in her name. It was not a project, but an outpouring of love to our friends on behalf of our friend, Donna. For many years now "Donna's Baskets" have literally touched thousands of lives, especially our own. We remember her, yes. But we also remember God's faithfulness to us in giving us all we need to bless others whom we love remembering, too.

Here is what her mom says: *"Donna never fully realized what a special 'somebody' she was to so many people and how she made such an impression on their lives. She often asked me, 'What am I good at anyway?' I saw her remembering the poor, the lonely, the 'different' person and going out of her way to do extra little things on birthdays or special days. Nothing was too much for her. Now that she sees things in a new light through eternity's eyes, she knows that what she considered insignificant acts of love, were God's way of remembering and encouraging others through her unique gift. So she* was *good at something."*

Sharing Our Hearts

Discussion Starters

Reflect on the following thoughts we will discuss together. Take particular note of those that strike a chord with you and add notes in the margin about them.

1. How do you want others to remember you? _____

   _____

   _____

   _____

   _____

   _____

   _____

2. The reality of death is not a popular or fun topic to discuss. It is usually talked about only when a loved one is facing death or has already died. Add to this list of what others have learned about dying.

   • "There was something about looking death in the face that enabled me to live life as God intends."

   • "Everyone will walk through this valley, but they do not need to walk it alone."

   • "God's comforting presence was with me. That surprised me."

   • "Others who came to my side brought great encouragement and it lifted the heaviness."

   • "Although my loved one died, I saw that I still had God's faithful love with me."

   • "I never knew a pain so great, but I also never knew so personal a relationship with God as in the months afterwards."

❑ other: _____

_____

_____

_____

_____

3. To be affectionately remembered by a friend deepens your relationship. What have you observed or concluded about remembering?

   ❑ It shows that there are no hard feelings.

   ❑ It is a beautiful, unselfish gift.

   ❑ It causes feelings of acceptance and closeness.

   ❑ It promotes trust and a desire to open up more freely.

   ❑ It creates a desire to do the same for others.

   ❑ other: _____

   _____

   _____

   _____

4. What do you remember of God's grace to you in your initial salvation experience?

   ❑ It surprised me with joy.

   ❑ It came when I least expected it through someone I never dreamed would bring it.

   ❑ It changed my life by _____

   _____

   ❑ It was so personal, tender, and, as the songwriter expresses it, amazing.

   ❑ It has never stopped and it keeps increasing.

❏ other: _____

_____

_____

5. It's amazing and sobering to think that God would reach out to us through other people, events, His Word, and His Spirit. Why would He do that?

❏ I really don't know. It's too hard to comprehend.

❏ so that I can in turn reach others

❏ because love always finds a way to re-establish a connection

❏ because He longs for relationship and intimacy with me

❏ other: _____

_____

_____

_____

_____

6. How do you feel about standing in line to suffer?

❏ It is not my favorite place to be.

❏ I do everything I can to avoid pain and suffering.

❏ I would never choose it, but I can learn great things from it.

❏ If I knew that the Lord Jesus was in line with me, I would do it more readily.

❏ other: _____

_____

_____

_____

_____

A Change of Heart

Lesson Summary and Application

One main thought I have gleaned from the lesson:

_____

_____

_____

_____

One application of this lesson to my life: With God's help . . .

- ❏ I will tell others more often of His grace to me.

- ❏ I will praise Him for saving me as a "somebody" and for valuing me.

- ❏ I will remember others I have neglected because of my selfishness.

- ❏ other: _____

_____

Walk the Word

- ❏ Get together with a friend over coffee and deliberately reminisce over experiences you have gone through together.

- ❏ Update your photo albums, thinking about God's hand in your life at all of the various stages.

- ❏ Visit a nursing home and invite a lonely resident to remember while you listen and appreciate.

- ❏ Remember a friend's birthday. Send her a card, and in it tell her what you appreciate most about her.

Notes

Hearing His Heart

The following verses on this week's topic, "A Friend Remembers," are given for deepening your love for the Lord and for others. Space is provided after each verse for you to record your thoughts.

WEEK 1

Monday

1 Chronicles 16:12

"_____ the wonders He has done."

_____

_____

_____

Tuesday

Isaiah 46:8-9

"_____ this, fix it in mind, take it to heart.... Remember the former things, those of long ago; I am God, and there is no other."

_____

_____

_____

Wednesday

Hebrews 8:12

"I will forgive their wickedness and will remember their _____ no more."

_____

_____

_____

Thursday

Psalm 111:4

"He has caused His _____ to be remembered;
the LORD is gracious and compassionate."

_____

_____

_____

Friday

Psalm 111:5

"He provides food for those who fear Him; He _____
his covenant forever."

_____

_____

_____

WEEK 2

Monday

Philippians 1:3

"I thank my God every time I _____ you."

_____

_____

_____

Tuesday

Romans 1:9

"God, whom I serve with my whole heart in preaching the
gospel of His Son, is my witness how constantly I remember you
in _____ ."

_____

_____

_____

Wednesday

Galatians 2:9-10

"James, Peter and John ... gave me and Barnabas the right hand of fellowship when they recognized the grace given to me. They agreed that we should go to the Gentiles, and they to the Jews. All they asked was that we should continue to remember _____ , the very thing I was eager to do."

_____

_____

_____

Thursday

Hebrews 13:3

"Remember those in prison as if _____ _____ , and those who are mistreated as if you yourselves were suffering."

_____

_____

_____

Friday

Malachi 3:16

"A scroll of_____ was written in His presence concerning those who feared the LORD and honored His name."

_____

_____

_____

CHAPTER 4

Mary Magdalene: Delivered and Directed

A Friend Lets Go

Amazing Grace

Amazing grace! How sweet the sound
That saved a wretch like me!
I once was lost, but now am found,
Was blind but now I see!

'Twas grace that taught my heart to fear,
And grace my fears relieved;
How precious did that grace appear
The hour I first believed.

Thru many dangers, toils and snares,
I have already come;
'Tis grace hath brought me safe thus far,
And grace will lead me home!

When we've been there ten thousand years,
Bright shining as the sun,
We've no less days to sing God's praise
Than when we'd first begun.

—John Newton

Scripture Reading: John 20:1-18

omen are gifted at making friends, for we are natural nurturers. But what does not typically come as easily is relinquishing, or letting go, which is also an essential part of a healthy, growing relationship. This process is usually joined by an unwelcome companion, Pain, and is therefore not a path we tend to delight in. Consequently, we do not spend a great deal of time talking about separation before it occurs. Parting is nevertheless a reality, and it is for our benefit, as well as for the benefit of our loved ones, to learn how to walk down this path with grace and dignity. But how can we do this? A look at the relationship between Jesus and His friend Mary Magdalene will give us a few insights.

Mary Magdalene, whom we will affectionately refer to as Maggy, is one of the lesser-known figures in Jesus' life, but that does not mean that she is less important than others. No indeed. The fact that she is the first to be entrusted with the message that Jesus is alive again reflects God's esteem for her. However, there is only one Scripture passage that tells us something about her life prior to the cross and the garden scenes. This passage in Luke 8:2 lets us in on two facts: Seven demons have been cast out of her, and she participates in a Friendship Circle® group that is helping to meet the practical needs of Jesus and His team of twelve during their time of ministry.

Delivered from Darkness

Both are very important pieces of information as we observe Maggy's encounter in the garden with Jesus (John 20). First, because of her past demon possession, it is likely that she has endured a great deal of fear, turmoil, and unbalanced thinking. Healthy relationships have not been known to her. She has been very disconnected from society and has experienced profound loneliness. Others have avoided her or outright rejected her. Who wants to be around someone who is full of lies, deceit, hatred, and turbulence?

But the passage tells us that Maggy has been freed from this debilitating possession. How awesome to reflect that the Lord Jesus in His mercy would reach down into her darkened heart and offer to illuminate it with Himself in such a personal and life-changing way! While previously she has existed in darkness, she can now revel in the ability to walk in the light. While her heart has been scarred by wounds of rejection, fear, and anxiety, she now finds herself not only accepted but dearly loved and constantly made aware of God's faithful care for her. It is only natural that she should long to return her love and appreciation to Jesus by joining this Friendship Circle® along with other women whose sole purpose is to serve Him.

As our scene opens we find Maggy threading her way toward the garden in the shadowy hours of the early morning. Few are out and about at this time, but we can only assume that, after the shattering events of the previous day, she has been unable to sleep. Unthinkable as it may seem, she must accept the reality that her friend Jesus has been brutally crucified. How her heart must ache, and every step she takes must be blurred by tears, as well as by the physical darkness, as she heads toward His tomb, accompanied by Pain.

Upon reaching her destination, though, Maggy is horrified at what she discovers. As though the situation were not bleak enough, it appears that someone has broken into the tomb and stolen the Lord's body! Maggy's first impulse is to do what any of us would under the circumstances. She seeks for help, stumbling back in the darkness to the support of her "Care Group" that includes Peter, John, and the other disciples. The baffled friends race back to the garden to verify her story. Then they return home, leaving Maggy, who has trailed back to the garden behind them, alone with her inconsolable grief.

Transforming Touch

What is Maggy to do? This is without a doubt the darkest hour of her life since before her deliverance from the horrible demons. She is crying. Where is Jesus now when she most needs Him? And so with a great weight of sadness, she begins searching for her Friend's missing body. Once again tears dampen her pathway as Maggy approaches the empty tomb. But wait! *Empty?* Are her eyes deceiving her? No—it is hardly empty. There is definitely somebody in there. Actually, there are at least two somebodies. Because as Maggy brushes away her tears, she clearly sees that she is about to be cast in a major role in "Touched By An Angel." She, who had been tortured by demons, is now to be personally comforted by angels.

Their placement in the picture is significant, and perhaps this is Maggy's first clue that she is on to something great. Seated at each end of the slab, the two angels exactly duplicate the picture given to Moses of the angels that hovered over the Ark in the Most Holy Place (Exodus 25:19). Here the repentant find mercy. Is she, too, about to receive God's mercy?

The angels speak to her, and their words are stirring and sensitive. *"Woman, why are you crying?"* (John 20:13). Are these not words of mercy to comfort any woman's broken heart? And the angels are not the only ones who cared enough to ask, because almost immediately the same question is asked by a Man whom Maggy thinks is the gardener: *"Woman, why are you crying? Who is it you are looking for?"* (John 20:15). Then the supposed gardener takes time to listen to her reply, after which He adds one more word that no stranger would know. Only a friend would. It is the one word that can reach Maggy in her desolation: *"Mary"* (John 20:16). And immediately she recognizes her Shepherd's voice. This is indeed the Lord Jesus. And He is *alive*, just as He had promised.

Not only is Jesus alive, but it would appear that He is interrupting His greatest mission of all time to stop and attend to Maggy's bleeding heart. How tenderly Jesus cares! He weeps with those who weep, and especially with His friends. *"Do not hold on to me, for I have not yet returned to the Father,"* He instructs. (John 20:17).

Letting Go and Letting God Direct

Then, along with His presence and words of comfort, Jesus gives her words of direction. The grieving need that. The Lord gently turns Maggy around, pointing out her new focus and ministry, helping her to face the reality that life has changed irrevocably for both of them. Instead of allowing her heart simply to cling to Jesus, the Teacher, she must now let go and view Him differently. Jesus has become the Eldest Brother of a larger family of faith (Romans 8:29).

Maggy is no longer alone in her sorrow, adrift without direction or purpose. Instead, because of Jesus' finished work and resurrection, she is now connected with the same Heavenly Father and brothers and sisters as He is. He has a job for her to do, and it begins by obeying His instructions: *"Do not hold on to me . . . Go instead to my brothers and tell them, 'I am returning to my Father and your Father, to my God and your God'"* (John 20:17). Jesus' mission of redemption has been accomplished, and His resurrection has proven it. That is indeed news worth sharing.

For Maggy, what looked like a burglary is transformed into an incredible blessing. What appeared to be an insurmountable crisis becomes a one-of-a-kind opportunity for caring and for allowing herself to be touched, not just by an angel, but by the Living God. For God's touch transforms. Maggy's heart and vision are enflamed anew as she runs from the garden exclaiming, *"I have seen the Lord"* (John 20:18).

Walking Arm in Arm

I am grateful for my sister, Maggy, who obeyed and did her job well. If she hadn't, we would not be reading her story. For all of us who belong to God's family of faith, we know that when separations come and we too lose something or someone who is very precious to us, we are at the same time gaining One even more precious. God gives us an awareness of His personal love for us through His Word, His Holy Spirit, and His Father's love expressed through the Body of Christ. We know that nothing, absolutely nothing, will ever be able to separate us from this ocean of love (Romans 8:39). And we are privileged to share this message of assurance with others. A whole new focus and ministry can begin as a result of our hearts being ignited with a passion for sharing the good news.

So come now, my dear sister. Let us walk together with grace and dignity as we take our Elder Brother's arm and proclaim to our world that we have a God who cares, comforts, forgives, and remembers.

A Modern Day Story
Pamela: A Friend Who Has Let Go

My friend Pamela has taught me a lot about letting go. She was willing to relinquish the comforts of home, possessions, and family to serve the Lord on the mission field. Then, after she had served there faithfully and sacrificially, making *it* her home, she was compelled to let go of the mission field several times to return temporarily to the States. So I asked her, "Pamela, tell me how in the world have you been able to let go of *everything*?"

She responded, *"There is only one place I want to be, and that is in the center of God's will. Nothing else really matters. When I stood by my dying mother's bedside, I saw afresh that there is nothing you take with you. People, pretty things, furniture, my glassware, and even the specific places where we minister—nothing matters but knowing and communing with God. Acts 20:24 tells me 'I consider my life worth nothing to me, if only I may finish the race and complete the task the Lord Jesus has given me— the task of testifying to the gospel of God's grace.' So I would rather have Jesus than any silver or gold. I'd rather be His than have riches untold. I'd rather have Him than houses or lands. I'd rather be led by his nail- scarred hands. For me, letting go has been agonizing and horrible at times. It breaks my heart, but I know God always has something better for me. And one of those better things is seeing God's heart and testifying of His grace and faithful provisions to me all day every day."*

I am so glad that Pamela's own life is not her most precious possession. She shares herself and the love of God willingly, shedding light in a dark world, and as a faithful friend she has touched many lives, including my own, in significant ways. Because she has learned to lean on Jesus, she models "letting go" with dignity and grace.

Sharing Our Hearts

Discussion Starters

Reflect on the following thoughts we will discuss together. Take particular note of those that strike a chord with you and add notes in the margin about them.

1. Does God ever let go of us? Explain your answer.

   _____

   _____

   _____

   _____

2. Healthy separations occur all through life. Which ones do you identify with most strongly, and how?

   ❏ a mom releasing her children

   ❏ a teacher facing graduation day

   ❏ a Care Circle member as the group completes its last chapter

   ❏ a friend with whom I no longer cross paths

   ❏ a wife whose husband is being transferred to another city.

   ❏ other: _____

   _____

   _____

   _____

   _____

   _____

   _____

   _____

3. We women are so good at clinging and trying to hold on to people forever. Why do you think we do that?

❑ We like security and the feeling of being loved.

❑ We resist change.

❑ We do not see the bigger picture, which is _____

_____

_____

_____

_____

_____

❑ Nurturing is part of our nature and we do it so well.

❑ We do not see what we have to offer to other people.

❑ We do not like to grieve or to be in the company of Pain.

❑ other: _____

_____

_____

_____

4. What can you do to make letting go less painful?

❑ admit that it will hurt for awhile

❑ cry

❑ talk about it

❑ pray, asking for God's help

❑ spend more time with God

❑ strengthen other relationships

❑ reach out to someone else who is hurting or lonely

❑ prepare for what is coming

❏ other: _____

_____

_____

_____

_____

5. Add to this list some benefits you see in letting go:

❏ It gives freedom to move in another direction.

❏ It is a testimony of growth for both parties.

❏ It frees our hands and arms to embrace someone or something new.

❏ It allows us to apply our wisdom and direct our love to work somewhere else.

❏ It shows that we believe in the person we are releasing.

❏ It enlarges our heart (and sometimes our pocketbook!).

❏ other: _____

_____

_____

_____

_____

A Change of Heart

Lesson Summary and Application

One main thought I have gleaned from the lesson:

_____

_____

_____

One application of this lesson to my life: With God's help . . .

❏ I will let go of _____

_____

_____

_____

❏ I will begin nurturing or sharing myself with _____

_____

_____

_____

❏ I will acknowledge that separation is going to hurt right now and I will allow myself to cry.

❏ other: _____

_____

_____

_____

_____

_____

Walk the Word

❏ Make it a point to reach out to a friend who has just experienced a separation.

❏ Observe the actions of people saying goodbye to one another in a busy airport.

❏ Send a card or an e-mail to a brother or sister in the faith and thank them for a kindness they have shown you.

Notes

Hearing His Heart

The following verses on this week's topic, "A Friend Lets Go," are given for deepening your love for the Lord and for others. Space is provided after each verse for you to record your thoughts.

WEEK 1

Monday

1 Samuel 1:22

"_____ and present him before the LORD, and he will live there always."

_____

_____

_____

Tuesday

Ecclesiastes 3:6

"[There is] a time to keep and a time to _____ ."

_____

_____

_____

Wednesday

Ruth 1:16

"Don't urge me to leave you or to turn back from you. Where you go _____, and where you stay _____. Your people will be my people and your God my God."

_____

_____

_____

Thursday

Psalm 63:7-8

"*Because you are my help, I sing in the shadow of your wings.
My soul _____ to you; your right hand upholds me.*"

_____

_____

_____

Friday

Deuteronomy 13:4

"*It is the LORD your God you must follow, and Him you must revere.
Keep His commands and obey Him; serve Him and _____
fast to Him.*"

_____

_____

_____

WEEK 2

Monday

Romans 8:35

"*Who shall _____ us from the love of Christ?*"

_____

_____

_____

Tuesday

Joshua 22:5

"*Be very careful to ... hold fast to Him and to serve Him with
_____ .*"

_____

_____

_____

Wednesday

Deuteronomy 30:19-20

"Now choose life, so that you and your children may live and that you may love the LORD your God, listen to His voice, and

_____ *."*

_____

_____

_____

Thursday

Philippians 3:12-14

"I press on to take hold of that for which Christ Jesus took hold of me.... One thing I do: _____

and straining toward what is ahead, I press on toward the goal to win the prize for which God has called me heavenward in Christ Jesus."

_____

_____

_____

Friday

Hebrews 13:5

"Never will I _____ *; never will I forsake you."*

_____

_____

_____

CHAPTER 5

Peter:
A Mess Turned Into
a Message of Mercy

A Friend Forgives

Just As I Am

*J*ust as I am, without one plea, but that Thy blood was shed for me,
And that Thou biddest me come to Thee, O Lamb of God, I come! I come!

*Just as I am, and waiting not, to rid my soul of one dark blot,
To Thee whose blood can cleanse each spot, O Lamb of God, I come! I come!*

*Just as I am, tho' tossed about with many a conflict, many a doubt,
Fightings and fears within, without; O Lamb of God, I come! I come!*

*Just as I am, poor, wretched, blind—sight, riches, healing of the mind,
Yea, all I need in Thee to find. O Lamb of God, I come! I come!*

*Just as I am, Thou wilt receive—wilt welcome, pardon, cleanse, relieve,
Because Thy promise I believe, O Lamb of God, I come! I come!*

—Charlotte Elliott

Scripture Reading: Luke 22:54-62

*M*any a relationship has been severed, not because harsh or caustic words have been spoken, a commitment neglected, or a confidence betrayed. Although these are indeed troubling and destructive occurrences, there is something far worse that can devastate a friendship or a marriage to the point that it can never be restored. A look at the life of Peter will give us insight into the identity of this insidious enemy and an effective way to deal with it.

Miraculous Ministry

Peter is a fervent man of faith, and as the early church is being established, he serves as its primary spokesman. The first time he stands up to preach, three thousand people come to Christ (Acts 2:41). But this stalwart rock has not always been strong in faith. Earlier on he had fluctuated between hot and cold in his dedication to the Lord Jesus. However, something dramatic has occurred to transform his fickle heart to one of unflinching commitment. What could this possibly be, and is it available to us today?

Peter, a fisherman, is introduced to Jesus at the outset of Jesus' public ministry and shortly afterward is selected as one of His twelve disciples who will walk and talk closely with Him. Peter abandons his fishing industry and undertakes a sacrificial ministry with Jesus of "fishing" for people. He shares with Jesus in a remarkable and exhilarating mission of teaching, preaching, feeding, and healing the sick and demon-possessed.

Over the course of their three-and-one-half years of shared ministry, a close bond develops between the two, as time after time Jesus entrusts His words and His heart to this outspoken and passionate individual. Peter shares his heart and pledges his undying loyalty to Jesus as well. His affection is clearly demonstrated in his unequivocal vow that he will never deny Jesus—never, ever. *"Even if all fall away on account of you, I never will,"* Peter brashly professes (Matthew 26:33), adding with a touch of dramatic confidence, *"Lord, I am ready to go with you to prison and to death"* (Luke 22:33).

Midnight Madness

But what Peter says and what Peter does are not always one and the same. As our story opens, a distraught Peter is warming himself by a campfire. It is the middle of the night, probably about 2:00 a.m., and he is trying to remain anonymous and nonchalant in unfamiliar and frightening circumstances.

Earlier in the evening he had attended an important dinner meeting with Jesus and the other eleven disciples in the upper room. Jesus had had many vital things to tell the somber group as they shared this unforgettable Passover meal, as well as serious personal instructions.

Following the meal Jesus and Peter, along with some of the others, had made their way to the Garden of Gethsemane for a serious prayer time. At least that was the intent, but that is not what happened in the garden. The sad reality is that Jesus had prayed alone while the disciples slept. They were *"exhausted from sorrow"* because of all that Jesus had shared with them (Luke 22:46), including the appalling revelation that one of the Twelve would betray Him (John 13:21).

Can you even imagine that? One of *them*! How could one of their very own close-knit band betray Jesus? Well, this will occur just as surely as another of their number will deny Him. And Peter is about to show them how.

Thanks to Judas, the midnight madness is now in full motion and there is no turning back. Jesus had been arrested, his disciples had scattered in panic, and Peter had headed toward a front row seat in the courtyard of the high priest where Jesus is being interrogated and will subsequently be condemned. Peter, despite his grief and confusion, has wanted to get a closer look at all that is going on.

As he warms himself by the fire, Peter becomes aware of a young servant girl who keeps staring inquisitively at him, and he starts to squirm. The warmth of the welcoming fire suddenly feels uncomfortably hot as she shares her observation with the gathered crowd: *"This man was with Him"* (Luke 22:56). Peter abruptly snaps back: *"Woman, I don't know Him"* (Luke 22:57). And within a very short period of time—a little over an hour—Peter twice more thoroughly and completely denies any connection with the Lord Jesus—his best friend.

As the third emphatic denial spews from Peter's lips, it draws the wordless attention of Jesus, who is at that very moment being taken away to be mocked, beaten, and tortured. The unmistakable and startling crow of a rooster pierces the night air. Jesus has only to turn and look, and His gaze reflects his heart of sorrow and forgiveness. As their eyes lock, Peter's emotions come spilling out.

His beloved Lord has both seen and heard his denials. But then, Jesus always sees and hears—and yet His love never wavers. Jesus understands that Peter's life does not match his high intentions.

Now, however, in this hour of crisis, this same realization finally impacts Peter profoundly. Indeed he has been all about talk rather than about walk.

A Broken Body and Broken Hearts

As that horrible truth settles into Peter's heart, it stings deeply, and he responds in a manner that is appropriate for a broken man: He weeps—and he weeps inconsolably (Luke 22:62).

Weeping in and of itself is not a wrong thing to do. Tears say much that cannot be expressed otherwise. Peter has been gifted in sharing, using words to convey his thoughts and feelings. But tears? Up to this point we haven't seen him shed any. But a deep cleansing has begun for Peter, and there is no holding back the flood of his repentance. Tears are a necessary response for a person learning to deny self and obey God instead of denying God and obeying self.

Peter comes to God with his broken heart. That is necessary for the deep inner healing of his broken soul. But more importantly, God will continue to approach Peter again and again.

Jesus, His body mutilated almost beyond recognition, shouldering His own cross, stumbles, stands, stoops, and finally stretches willing arms out to His executioners. No nails are needed to hold Him to the cross, but the soldiers hammer the nails through His flesh anyway. Then they raise His cross and continue to mock Him mercilessly.

Jesus hangs His head in hideous disgrace as He becomes the innocent guilt offering for the sins of the whole world. With drooping fingers, unclenched fists, and outstretched arms, He signs for all of deaf mankind, "I love you." He cries to His Father, the sun ceases to shine, women wail, the Father frowns, the ground grumbles, and the Son's heart and side spurt blood—and forgiveness.

A soldier, whose heart has been deeply stirred, interprets this sign language and worships, *"Surely this man was the Son of God!"* (Mark 15:39). Finally the Lord's broken, bruised, bloody, and battered body is bundled and buried. Shock waves reverberate and settle in on those who have loved the sacrificial Lamb. Lips and tomb are sealed tightly, seemingly never to be opened again. Sin has seen its finest night.

Marvelous Mercy

But *grace*, not *sin*, is the final word, and three days later in the early dawn Grace comes calling at the tomb, ringing resurrection bells. Jesus' crowning hour has arrived, and as joy bells ring in concert, the dead rise up to listen, the fearful become faithful, and the scattered are regathered. Once again, the Lord Jesus walks, talks, and eats with those who love Him most.

Peter is among the first to whom Jesus pays a visit (Luke 24:34). Jesus could have gone back to Pilate, the soldiers, or the High Priests, but true to His character, He comes close to the one whose heart has been tenderized by tears (Psalm 34:18). He shares His own heart once again with his close friend. Friends do that, you know. They connect.

Days later, around a campfire, Jesus looks once again into Peter's eyes, but this time the penetrating look is welcomed. Jesus invites this melted heart, not just once, but three times, to feed His sheep (John 21:15-17). He continues to be unconditionally accepting of Peter and commissions him to minister to His people.

Peter clasps the scepter of grace extended from Jesus' nail-scarred hands, and forgiveness flows freely. From that day forward Peter, mindful of such marvelous mercy and grace, changes his inconsistent ways and becomes a rock on which others can lean. They too, through Peter, will hear God's message of mercy.

Peter receives not what he deserves but what he needs: a restored relationship, a humbled heart, and a job to do—to pass along God's mercy to those who have messed up their lives.

Yes, denial is hurtful, betrayal is horrible, slanderous words are cruel, and broken promises crushing. But even in the face of the worst mistreatment, if we do not demonstrate an attitude of unconditional love and forgiveness, our own sin is equally great. Jesus Christ has loved us unconditionally and has forgiven us for far more than we can imagine. He is the only One who has the right to take offense, yet He chooses to forgive. Grace stands ready to make a house call.

Excuse me. I think I hear a doorbell. What about you?

A Modern Day Story
Diana: A Friend Who Is Forgiving

My friend Diana shared with me the other day that she has made the choice to forgive a lot of people during her lifetime. My ears pricked right up as she continued: *"One of the most important ones was my father. When my mom and he divorced, he was not part of my life at all, and actually I was glad. He had done many things to me that were unkind. For years I ignored him so that he could not hurt me anymore. Then one day, as clear as a bell, the thought came to me that I was no better than my dad. I was being mean to him by keeping him out of my life. So I sent him a letter on Father's Day and told him that I wanted to see him and talk to him. One day I came home from work and there he was in the living room. I started crying and said, 'Daddy, would you forgive me for all the ways I have hurt you?' He said to me, 'I should be asking you for forgiveness.' A little while after that he died, and I was very glad that we had reconciled."* We talked a little more and then Diana added, *"There is something in our spirits that cannot rest until we are restored. I believe God has put it there for us to be reconciled to Him and to others."*

Sharing Our Hearts

Discussion Starters

Reflect on the following thoughts we will discuss together. Take particular note of those that strike a chord with you and add notes in the margin about them.

1. Do you think that God still makes house calls today? Explain your answer.

   _____

   _____

   _____

   _____

2. Someone has said that forgiveness is a gift that you give your-self. In what ways has this been true for you?

   ❏ I am free to love and to spend time with the other person again.

   ❏ I have more joy because my mind is not flooded with negative thoughts.

   ❏ I can embrace and enjoy more blessings today because I am no longer living in the past.

   ❏ I am less tired, since holding grudges tends to sap energy and adversely affect health.

   ❏ I feel better about myself and others because my burden has been rolled away.

   ❏ other: _____

   _____

   _____

   _____

3. We all make mistakes. What are some of the positives you can take away from these experiences?

❑ learn from them

❑ correct what I am able to correct

❑ ask for forgiveness, when appropriate

❑ forgive myself and move on

❑ continue to take more risks

❑ pray, asking God for His forgiveness and help

❑ accept the fact that I am human and I make mistakes

❑ other: _____

_____

_____

_____

4. How do you hurt others?

❑ I ignore or judge them.

❑ I promise one thing and do another.

❑ I fail to apologize or seek reconciliation.

❑ I don't try to see another's point of view.

❑ I neglect to reach out warmly.

❑ I am insensitive to their needs.

❑ I don't ask them how they are or how I can help them.

❑ other: _____

_____

_____

_____

_____

5. Why do you not always want to "walk the talk"?

❏ Sometimes it is very hard to do.

❏ I am more self-focused than God- or others-focused.

❏ It can require a lot of effort and energy.

❏ I don't see the importance of it.

❏ I think I can manage my life in my own strength.

❏ other: _____

_____

_____

_____

A Change of Heart

Lesson Summary and Application

One main thought I have gleaned from the lesson:

_____

_____

_____

_____

One application of this lesson to my life: With God's help . . .

❏ I will be true to my word.

❏ I will choose to honor God and others more.

❏ I will forgive myself for the mistakes I have made.

❏ other: _____

_____

_____

Walk the Word

❏ Forgive someone in your heart for something that has happened a long time ago, even if you have for all practical purposes already put the deed behind you. Observe whether the quality of your relationship is affected. Consider approaching this person, apologizing, and then asking, "What can I do to help correct this?"

❏ If there is a child in your life, make it a point to give him or her a second chance after necessary discipline. Be sincere in your praise for success.

❏ Observe a service person, clerk, or waitress who has made a mistake. Are they willing to acknowledge the error, or do they prefer to brush it off? If you are impressed with the way they handled the situation let them know.

Notes

Hearing His Heart

The following verses on this week's topic, "A Friend Forgives," are given for deepening your love for the Lord and for others. Space is provided after each verse for you to record your thoughts.

WEEK 1

Monday

Luke 17:3

"If your brother sins, _____ , and if he repents, _____ ."

_____

_____

_____

Tuesday

Ephesians 4:32

"Be kind and compassionate to one another, _____ each other, just as in Christ God forgave you."

_____

_____

_____

Wednesday

Colossians 3:12-13

" ... clothe yourselves with compassion, kindness, humility, gentleness and patience. Bear with each other and _____ whatever grievances you may have against one another. Forgive as the Lord forgave you."

_____

_____

_____

Thursday

Luke 11:4

"_____ us our sins, for we also _____ everyone who sins against us."

_____

_____

_____

Friday

Matthew 6:14-15

"If you _____ men when they sin against you, your heavenly Father will also forgive you. But if you do not forgive men their sins, your Father will not forgive your sins."

_____

_____

_____

WEEK 2

Monday

Proverbs 24:29

"Do not say, 'I'll do to him as _____ ; I'll pay that man back for what he did.'"

_____

_____

_____

Tuesday

Luke 23:34

"Jesus said, 'Father, _____ , for they do not know what they are doing.'"

_____

_____

_____

_____

Wednesday

Daniel 9:9

"The LORD our God is merciful and _____ ."

_____

_____

_____

Thursday

Luke 6:37

"Forgive and you will be _____ ."

_____

_____

_____

Friday

Luke 7:47

"Her many sins have been _____ —for she loved much."

_____

_____

_____

CHAPTER **6**

Paul:
A Hit Man
Captured by God

A Friend Is Faithful

Where He Leads Me

I can hear my Savior calling,
I can hear my Savior calling;
I can hear my Savior calling,
"Take thy cross and follow, follow me."

I'll go with Him thru the garden,
I'll go with Him thru the garden;
I'll go with Him thru the garden,
I'll go with Him, with Him all the way.

He will give me grace and glory,
He will give me grace and glory;
He will give me grace and glory,
And go with me, with me all the way.

Chorus:
Where He leads me I will follow,
Where He leads me I will follow;
Where He leads me I will follow,
I'll go with Him, with Him all the way.

—E. W. Blandly

Scripture Reading: Acts 9:1-19

ow do you know that someone is a person of integrity and therefore worthy of your trust? Many claim to be loyal friends and business partners, but over time their actions prove differently. Most of us do not desire to take the lesser path, but sadly we sometimes compromise. How can we be assured that we are on the road to becoming people of integrity and that over time we will be worthy of the trust and friendship of others? A look at the early life of a great apostle—someone who had thought that he was so right but was in fact living so wrongly—illustrates this situation for us and demonstrates the relevance of the cross to our lives.

The greatest missionary who has ever lived, apart from the Lord Jesus Himself, was a man who knew at the very core of his being the meaning of the cross. He lived the cross and died for it. But he had not always believed it. There was a time, as there has been for each of us, when he was spiritually blind and ignorant. No one at the time could have convinced Saul of that. As far as he was concerned, he was a man of sterling integrity. He had been schooled thoroughly in the Jewish ways, was a devout religious leader, and was exceptionally zealous in preserving the traditional values of the Pharisee sect to which he belonged. But was he really someone faithful, true, and trustworthy?

It depends on whom you might ask. If you were to ask the man himself, Saul would affirm this with a resounding yes, because he was sincere in his hatred of Christians and aware of no major sins in his own life. He was in fact notably proud of his record in the sin category. But if you were to have asked God the same question about Saul, He would have had the opposite answer. His measuring stick of integrity is not based on sincerity alone but on truth—the truth taught, caught, and dwelling in His Son, Jesus. Saul was far from following Truth, although that was going to change drastically in the very near future. Granted, it would take extreme measures to get him to see the light, but then Grace delights in going the extra mile and showing up when least expected.

Hit Man Strikes Again

Saul, self-appointed hit-man for the Jews, is leaving town on a mission to track down, beat, imprison, and persecute disciples of Jesus Christ. On this particular day he is heading toward Damascus on a search for these "heretics" who have gone far beyond the fringe of orthodox Judaism. Saul has secured the necessary search warrants from his superiors in order to keep all proceedings clean and legal. Now, equipped with a knapsack filled with handcuffs, he is off with his cohorts on the day's mission.

With no advance warning Saul and his traveling companions are literally knocked off their feet—hit broadside by a megaforce of flashing light—and then a Voice breaks the silence, a Voice that only Saul can understand. It becomes instantaneously clear to this murderous young man exactly who is on the Most Wanted List.

Saul, the relentless head-hunter, has suddenly become the hunted. There can be no denying that Someone is out to get him and that there is no escaping His grip. A simultaneous hit of power and light would cause quite a jolt to anyone's system. This is certainly the case for Saul, and he is instantly blinded.

Saul, despite his shock, faces the reality that he has been rendered powerless, that his mission trip is over, and that his very life is at stake—there can be no telling where, when, or how that power and light will zap again. And like the good student he is, *he pays attention.* Specifically, he listens to this Voice: *"Saul, Saul, why do you persecute me?"* (Acts 9:4).

Saul's mind must be flooded with answers (and questions), but only one response, a question of his own, comes out. He articulates this all-important question with an open mind and with great respect: *"Who are you, Lord?"* (Acts 9:5). Saul has not recognized Jesus' voice because he has not yet made His acquaintance.

For a man or woman to be so honest before God as to admit *"I don't know you,"* and to be ready at the same time to begin a personal journey to change—that is a crowning moment. Lack of relationship with God is the wisest admission anyone can ever make. Difficult? Yes. Humbling? Indeed. But oh, so necessary!

He who thinks he knows something in reality knows nothing until he learns and accepts the truth of the Lord Jesus. This truth sets a person free (John 8:32). Saul does exactly this, and the dialogue between these soul-brothers is established and is to continue throughout the remainder of Saul's life on earth and beyond.

The Voice continues, *"I am Jesus, whom you are persecuting.... Now get up and go into the city, and you will be told what you must do"* (Acts 9:6). God has a personal message that He will deliver to Saul later. Right now though, Saul needs to recognize that, despite his overwhelming guilt, his life has been spared. Ultimately, one does not persist in persecuting or rejecting Jesus, Almighty God, and get away with it. There is a judgment day for those who do. But God's patience is unlimited, and at this particular moment, He is offering Saul His incredible, undeserved mercy. It is the same mercy He is offering both the Jews and the Gentiles, and Saul comes to at least a beginning of understanding of this reality with his first-hand encounter with the Savior.

Captured by God

From that moment on, Saul is a transformed man. Upon leaving the scene of the incident, he is led, helpless, into the very city in which he had intended to arrest others, and he instead places himself in solitary confinement. For three days Saul eats and drinks nothing. His world has been turned upside down, and he needs to come to terms with the implications of his new vision of reality.

Finally, a disciple in Damascus who could have been arrested by Saul now comes at the Spirit's bidding and blesses Saul. What faith Ananias has! The blessing results in healing for Ananias's former mortal enemy—both inwardly and outwardly. He is also given a clear direction, and he is already well on his way to becoming a man of integrity in God's eyes.

Saul, later to be called Paul, accepts the calling to bring others out of the kingdom of darkness into the kingdom of light, but this decision is going to cost him dearly. The road will be hard and narrow. The mission will not be merely inconvenient, but sacrificial, but Saul is equipped for the task because he has seen the love of His Savior. Carrying out his new vision will require integrity: He will have to remain faithful and true to God and to his own word, whatever the cost.

Whereas Saul has in the past taken seriously his "mission" of persecuting Christians, he now takes seriously the preaching of the cross of Christ, proclaiming boldly that all *"should repent and turn to God and prove their repentance by their deeds"* (Acts 26:20). This is a powerful, life-changing message, but it is one that will nevertheless be strongly resisted.

In order to hold firm to his teaching about the cross and the resurrection of Christ, Paul will have to oppose his own Jewish brothers and will find himself the one persecuted and imprisoned. He will be flogged; whipped; beaten with rods; stoned; shipwrecked; lost at sea; and in danger from rivers, bandits, his own Jewish countrymen, the Gentiles, and false "brothers." In addition, no matter where he travels or lives he will find himself homeless, hungry, cold, inadequately clothed, weary, worn out, and weak (2 Corinthians 11:23-29). Rejection, hostility, and suffering will be close and constant traveling companions.

On the other hand, Paul will become more and more intimately acquainted with Jesus, his Lord and Savior. Who would not want to know well the One who loves them best? Paul's consistent heart cry will be: *"I want to know Christ and the power of his resurrection and the fellowship of sharing in his sufferings, becoming like Him in His death"* (Philippians 3:10).

Committed to the Cross

The idea of becoming like Jesus *in his death* is not one the world promotes. To die to one's own selfishness, take up one's cross, and follow the Lord Jesus wherever He may lead sounds like a foreign language to most in our world—and sadly enough often to our church community as well. We'd much prefer to promote ourselves and look out for "Number One." We'd rather be sumptuously fed than to feed others. We'd rather defend our rights, our positions, or our programs than to suffer silently and wait on God to make changes in people's hearts. We'd much prefer to be served than to serve, to receive than to give, to be prayed for than to intercede in prayer, to nurse a grudge than to forgive, to study God's Word than to live it. We would rather focus on our own pain than take steps to listen or to reach out a hand of encouragement to a suffering sister or brother.

If we are, however, to be people of integrity, worthy of others' trust and friendship over the long haul, then they must see that we walk our talk all day, every day. The world must know that when we say we are going to do something we *will* do it. And those around us must observe that we continue to move closer to Jesus, loving sacrificially as He loves, and praying sincerely, "Please help me to be more like you, whose name is called *'Faithful and True'*" (see Revelation 19:11)— not just in the big things, but in the little things, as well.

A Modern Day Story
Bill: A Pastor Who Is Faithful

Recently I spoke with Pastor Bill, a seasoned pastor with almost sixty years of experience behind the pulpit. I wanted to know how he had learned faithfulness. His is an impressive record—not an easy thing to accomplish. I know that his pastoral life has been unusually challenging and full of sorrows.

I was privileged to hear his little sermon: *"I learned faithfulness from the Word and from attending church every week. When I came to the Lord as a teenager, my pastor taught us to go to church regularly. It was not an option in those days once you became a Christian. We went because at church we were taught the Word and that the Lord must be first. The Word teaches that faithfulness is a fruit of the Spirit (Galatians 2:20). It is the name of the Rider in Revelation 19:11—'Faithful and True.' It is the Holy Spirit who is our Comforter and never leaves us or forsakes us. So it is the very nature of God Himself—His essence. Proverbs says a faithful man abounds with blessing. Actually, if a Christian does not have faithfulness or integrity he hardly has anything else that amounts to any good. I ache to see how many Christians do not keep their word and how the church suffers because of it."*

I thanked Pastor Bill and shared with him that his words reminded me of those of Paul the apostle. He began to share his opinion of Paul as the most faithful man of all—and sermon number two was well on its way. It was as worthwhile as the first!

Sharing Our Hearts

Discussion Starters

Reflect on the following thoughts we will discuss together. Take particular note of those that strike a chord with you and add notes in the margin about them.

1. Name a friend who has always been faithful to you:

   _____

   How does his or her faithfulness make you feel? _____

   _____

2. What does it mean to you to deny yourself and carry your cross today?

   ❏ that I live a life of thankfulness to God for His grace

   ❏ that I pursue God, not money or popularity or beauty

   ❏ that I give up things in order to be with Him

   ❏ that I might live in a more humble home than I'd prefer

   ❏ that I might find myself in a position of having to reduce my spending in order to have more to give to God and to others

   ❏ that I will in many instances need to do what is inconvenient and costly

   ❏ other: _____

   _____

   _____

   _____

   _____

3. Paul later admitted that he had in his early adulthood "acted in ignorance and unbelief" (1 Timothy 1:13). In what ways do you do the same?

❏ when I am insensitive to others' feelings and hurt them by:

_____

_____

_____

_____

❏ when I refuse to consider any viewpoint other than my own

❏ when I am closed-minded and refuse to discuss an issue

❏ when I consider my own circumstances more than I focus on God

❏ when I do not have eternity's values in view

❏ other: _____

_____

_____

_____

_____

_____

_____

4. When you commit to following Christ, what might you realistically expect?

❏ Others might not understand my decision.

❏ I might at times need to stand alone.

❏ I will be in the minority.

❏ I will enjoy a sweet fellowship with Jesus Christ.

❏ I will need to rearrange my life and schedule for the sake of others.

❏ It will cost me something: _____

_____

❏ other: _____

_____

_____

_____

_____

_____

_____

5. Why does the world think of the cross as foolishness?

❏ It makes one vulnerable and allows others to take advantage.

❏ It makes more sense to many to earn and save a lot of money.

❏ A prevalent idea is that being important equates to being famous or well-known.

❏ People don't want to think about an afterlife.

❏ Many consider it foolish to give away what one has worked hard for.

❏ People fail to recognize God's mercy and grace toward them.

❏ other: _____

_____

_____

_____

_____

_____

A Change of Heart

Lesson Summary and Application

One main thought I have gleaned from the lesson:

_____

_____

_____

_____

One application of this lesson to my life: With God's help . . .

❏ I will be faithful and true to my word.

❏ I will focus on God and on loving others instead of focusing on myself.

❏ I will move closer to those God is asking me to love by:

_____

_____

❏ other: _____

_____

_____

Walk the Word

❏ Make a special point of keeping a promise you have made to God or to someone else.

❏ If you have children, commend them for a specific way they are demonstrating their faithfulness to God.

❏ Go out of your way to show an unexpected kindness to a neighbor or friend.

Notes

Hearing His Heart

The following verses on this week's topic, "A Friend Is Faithful,"
are given for deepening your love for the Lord and for others.
Space is provided after each verse for you to record your
thoughts.

WEEK 1

Monday

Matthew 25:23

"Well done, good and _____ servant!"

_____

_____

_____

Tuesday

Psalm 101:6

"My eyes will be on the _____ in the land."

_____

_____

_____

Wednesday

2 Thessalonians 3:3

*"The Lord is _____ , and He will
strengthen and protect you from the evil one."*

_____

_____

_____

Thursday

Revelation 2:10

"Be _____ , even to the point of death, and
I will give you the crown of life."

_____

_____

_____

Friday

Joshua 24:14

"Now _____ the LORD and _____ Him with
all faithfulness."

_____

_____

_____

WEEK 2

Monday

Psalm 117:2

"For great is His love toward us, and the _____
of the LORD endures forever."

_____

_____

_____

Tuesday

3 John 3

"It gave me great joy to have some brothers come and tell about
your faithfulness to _____ ."

_____

_____

_____

Wednesday

Psalm 119:90

"Your _____ *continues through all generations.*"

_____

_____

_____

Thursday

Lamentations 3:22-23

"Because of the LORD's great love we are not _____ *, for His compassions never fail. They are new every morning; great is your* _____."

_____

_____

_____

Friday

Proverbs 28:20

"A faithful man will be _____."

_____

_____

_____

Prayer Journal

Lesson 1   Date _____

PRAISES

_____
_____
_____
_____
_____
_____
_____
_____
_____
_____

PETITIONS

_____
_____
_____
_____
_____
_____
_____
_____
_____
_____

Prayer Journal

Lesson 2   Date _____

PRAISES

_____
_____
_____
_____
_____
_____
_____
_____
_____
_____

PETITIONS

_____
_____
_____
_____
_____
_____
_____
_____
_____
_____
_____

Prayer Journal

Lesson 3   Date _____

PRAISES

_____
_____
_____
_____
_____
_____
_____
_____
_____

PETITIONS

_____
_____
_____
_____
_____
_____
_____
_____
_____

Prayer Journal

Lesson 4   Date _____

PRAISES

_____
_____
_____
_____
_____
_____
_____
_____
_____

PETITIONS

_____
_____
_____
_____
_____
_____
_____
_____
_____
_____

Prayer Journal

Lesson 5   Date _____

PRAISES

_____
_____
_____
_____
_____
_____
_____
_____
_____
_____

PETITIONS

_____
_____
_____
_____
_____
_____
_____
_____
_____
_____
_____

Prayer Journal

Lesson 6   Date _____

PRAISES

_____
_____
_____
_____
_____
_____
_____
_____
_____
_____

PETITIONS

_____
_____
_____
_____
_____
_____
_____
_____
_____
_____

Note to the Reader

The publisher invites you to share your response to the message of this book by writing Discovery House Publishers, P.O. Box 3566, Grand Rapids, MI 49501, USA or by calling 1-800-653-8333. For information about other Discovery House publications, contact us at the same address and phone number. Find us on the Internet at http://www.dhp.org/ or send e-mail to books@dhp.org.

The design of this study guide is based on the tools used in the ministry of Friendship Circle® International. If you would like more information please contact: Friendship Circle® International, P.O. Box 2062, Renton, WA 98056.